Anonymous

Uncle Sam's Visit to the U. S. Senate

Anonymous

Uncle Sam's Visit to the U. S. Senate

ISBN/EAN: 9783743377899

Manufactured in Europe, USA, Canada, Australia, Japa

Cover: Foto ©ninafisch / pixelio.de

Manufactured and distributed by brebook publishing software
(www.brebook.com)

Anonymous

Uncle Sam's Visit to the U. S. Senate

TO

THE PRESENT

DEMOCRATIC CONGRESS,

THAT NOBLE BAND OF NEW-STYLE

PATRIOTS, WHOSE SYMPATHIES ARE SO

BROAD AS TO INCLUDE EVEN THEIR OWN POCKETS

AND THEMSELVES; AND WHOSE CALM AND

BENIGN INTELLIGENCE HAS ENABLED

THEM TO EVOLVE THE FOLLOW-

ING NEW POLITICAL

MAXIM:

"TO DO NOTHING IS SAFER SOMETIMES THAN TO DO

SOMETHING,"

THIS LITTLE BOOK IS RESPECTFULLY DEDICATED.

The thought struck me some days ago,
Perchance the world would like to know
About the visit that was made—
(True! without any great parade)
By Uncle Sam who went to see
His servants who serve Liberty;
When, harvest season being done,
He thought he'd see the goings-on
At a place called Washington.
For having read the daily papers,
He had heard about the capers
That the Senate had been playing,
Whilst he had been to work at haying;
But when the hay at last was stacked,
Said Uncle Sam; "Now I'll be cracked,
If I don't jest go down and see,
About this 'ere tom-foolery,
Thet folks say is taking place,
In the law shop o' the race.
I don't know what's up, I am sure,
But politicks must be kept pure;
So guess I'll have to take a peek,
To see ef I kin find a leak."
So, laying out some shirts and collars,
Two pair of socks, and eighty dollars
Which he with thrift had laid away,

To serve him 'gainst a rainy day,
And seizing his old carpet sack,
Uncle Sam began to pack.
And having packed, with grip in hand,
From his farm house in the North
Uncle Sam set gaily forth,
Toward the line of Dixie Land,
To see the town he used to know,
About a century ago.
He reached there safely, and straightway
Stowing his old grip away,
And having washed his hands and face,
He took a look around the place.
Nobody knew him there and so
He had a good time, you must know,
In getting at the ins and outs,
Of the scenery there-abouts.
With things that are and are not sainted
He at length became acquainted,
By following strictly, I may say,
The usual senatorial way,
Of taking a quiet interest in ,
All living things from stocks to tin.
'Twas thus, alas, one eve while he
Was pondering in perplexity,
That Uncle Samuel was fated
To see the things herein related.

Uncle Sam's Visit to the U. S. Senate

Upon the broad Potomac's shore,
    One somber Autumn day,
With his hands thrust in his pockets,
    In a manly sort of way,
Uncle Samuel stood thinking
    Beside the silver sea,
And his visage was as rueful,
    As ruefulness can be.
He was thinking how the statesmen
    Of a certain Yankee Nation,
After long and dreary months
    Of steady legislation, —
Or rather ages after 'twas
    Supposed to have begun, —
Had talked about ten million things
    And not done a blessed one.

The more the plain and simple facts
   Rose before his inner eyes,
The more he felt down in his heart
   All his pent-up dander rise:—
Said he, " By thunderation, I'm
   Agoin' to swear by dang;
I vow I've got to take a hand
   And run my own shebang:—
If that Senate don't do something
   About this thing o' pelf,
I'm blamed if I don't regulate
   The pesky laws myself."
So saying, Uncle Samuel
   (Full name United States)
Passed slowly up behind the house,
   And through the White House gates;
He watched the leaves a-falling;
   He watched the skies turn blue,
While he seemed to be a-making
   Up his mind what he would do.

"I'm agoin' to swear, by dang."

But presently he spruced up as
    Some ladies passed him by,
He took a look to see the time;
    He gazed back at the sky;
Then up the street went striding
    At a nervous swinging gait,
Straight to the haughty columns where
    The Senate sits in state;
He turned in towards the marble steps
    Where the statue stood,
When looking up he murmured slow
    In a reflective mood, —
"I wonder if live Senators
    Ever have been good;
Or is the fiction really fact,
    As it has been said,
That Senators are only good
    After they are dead.
Ah! if George or Thomas J—
    Should come back here to-day,

I wonder what our Democrats
　　Would have the face to say;
I wonder now if Thomas
　　Would really understand,
That this is still the U. S.,
　　And not some foreign land."
So pondering many musings
　　Within his busy brain,
Uncle Samuel went poking
　　'Long with the crowded train
Of people who were climbing up
　　To see what they could see,
In that prize show place for humor—
　　The Senate Gallery.

The other folks went in at once,
　　But just as he came near,
The guardian shouted loudly:
　　"There's no more room in here!"'
Uncle Samuel said something
　　That sounded much like damn,

And then informed that fellow
  That his name was Uncle Sam.
The keeper said that he was very
  Very glad to know his name,
But he wouldn't let no hayseed
  Bulldoze him just all the same.
A looker-on then asked him
  If he didn't have a pull,
While the keeper kept saying
  That the Senate was all full.
So Uncle Sam went hustling
  'Round to another door,
Which somehow he thought he reckoned
  He hadn't seen before;
But just as he was going in,
  Somebody wished to know,—
Where that poor old country jake
  Thought he was tryin' to go!

His clothes were rather shabby—
  You must remember that;

His boots smelt of the country;
  Likewise his old plug hat;
His hair was not so quiet
  As a city dandy's is,
While unshaved sproutings covered
  That good old face of his;
He was a mite upset no doubt;
  His head was in a maze;
But what seemed most against him
  Was his plain old-fashioned ways;
Yet he managed somehow to blurt out:—
  "I've been here before;
I want to hear the silver''—
  And then he said no more;
At the single, small word "Silver"—
  Lo! straightway betide,
He stood within the Senate
  For the door had opened wide.
Then he sat him in a corner
  As quiet as could be,

And next he took a look around
  To see what he could see.

Below him there the Senators—
  Those sentinels of fate—
Calmly sat in sleeping rows
  Nodding to the great debate,
As standing, talking to the air
  Upon two stalwart feet,
Someone would say his something,
  And then start to repeat.
As Uncle Sam sized up the place,
  He muttered, ''Well, by gum;
I'm confounded if I ain't glad
  After all now that I come.
This is the nice way, —is it ?
  By all old freedom's guns,
That the whole fly-wheel machinery
  Of my government runs!
Well, well, this is a circus
  That I never would have missed;

An' to think those chaps get salaries
  For a doin' of all this!''
He leaned him o'er the railing,
  Where in calm and peaceful sleep
Two bulky Senators were trying
  Most gracefully to keep
Their gentle equilibrium;
  Just to show how things should be;
And from appearance were succeeding
  Unto a perfect T.
Another pair were smiling up
  Like two empty headed dudes,
While the rest were sort of strewed around
  In various attitudes.
A paper here; a letter there;
  Some reading and some writing,—
They were an all-fired motley crowd
  And not quite all inviting;
A pair of boots would upward soar
  As if they'd reach the ceiling;

Another pair would dig the floor.
  As if it had no feeling;
While some were scribbling letters
  In a perfect raging fury,
Some looked calm as if there wasn't
  Such a mortal thing as hurry.
One would tiptoe to his neighbor
  To say a little word;
Another'd sit like Egypt's Sphinx
  That has never stirred;
Thus while some were whispering;
  Some snoozing and some walking,
An orator in front would be
  Trying to do his talking.
Amidst the buzz of conversation;
  The whizzing of the air—
And a sort of mixed up mess of sounds
  That came from everywhere,
A faint and mellow music
  That seemed very like a snore,

Was wafted in gentle anthems
    Up from the Senate floor.
'Twas a corporatious Senator
    Whose dreams must have been bad,
For he snorted like a harpooned whale,
    When it's starting to get mad,
Then suddenly his big fat head
    Began to toss and roll,
As if his visions weren't
    Exactly soothing to his soul.
While the status which he had
    So carefully maintained,
Became a little shaky—
    I may say a little strained —
For with a most amazing snort
    And one last troubled snore
He woke—in time to save himself
    From rolling on the floor.
Uncle Sam burst out a-laughing
    With a hearty ha! ha! he!

"Twas a corporations' Senator

He laughed until the rafters shook
In that Senate Gallery;
"Wal, now, I say that that performance
Was pretty middlin' good;
He didn't fall,—but Lordy!
I was hopin' that he would!"

With chubby fists that member
Rubbed his eyes—then rubbed again;
Next sat up and looked about
In haughty, proud disdain;
He seemed to feel somehow deep down
An inward consciousness,
That he had run some awful risk—
Though what he could not guess;
But far down in his mind indeed
There plainly seemed to be,
A need just then of keeping up
Some extra dignity.
For after that, save now and then
For a blank-eyed sleepy blink,

And one or two back-sliding nods
   Mixed with a dreamy wink,
That Senator he sat bolt up
   And no member you could see,
Was half as wide awake (outside)
   As that member seemed to be.
While Uncle Sam was watching him
   Of the corporatious snore,
Another member sprang in haste
   Upon the Senate floor,—
"I rise to point of order!
   I am sorry but I fear
That though this Senate seems in session,
   There is no quorum here!"
Applause arose from all the friends
   Of said sorrow-stricken man,
While wrath filled those who think their friends
   Should slumber while they can.
The Speaker spoke: "The Clerk will please
   Proceed to call the roll."

And then 'twas found they needed two
　To make their quorum whole.

Hurry scurry went the Sergeant,
　And soon he brought in one;
Then another one was captured
　As he was trying to run.
But neither of them seemed to have
　The slightest spark of shame,
About the thing of going in
　And answering to their name.
The roll was called once more,
　But one—whom everybody knew—
When the Clerk called out his name,
　Wouldn't say as much as booh.
They tried to make him answer,
　But he sat and just kept mum,
Looking calm and quite collected,
　And mighty all-fired dumb.
Then the Speaker said that Mr. X.
　Might not answer to his name,

But the Senate would proceed
   With its business just the same.
Then Mr. X. who hadn't answered
   Because he didn't choose,
Now began orating like
   A mill-dam broken loose.
His face all flushed with crimson,
   Grew redder and more red,
And this is a small sample of what
   That noble member said :
(He was a chap who tipped the scales
   At a good two-hundred weight)
"Mr. Speaker, 'tis with sorrow
   That herewith I rise to state,
That since I didn't answer when
   The clerk read that roll-call,
It showed—why it just showed I reckon
   That I wasn't here at all ! "
With a calm beatified expression
   On his expansive face,

He squeezed himself back in his seat
   With a cute unconscious grace
A fellow member rose and said :
   " Now it seems to me he was—
Being here don't show his presence—
   Well, I rather guess it does! "
The Speaker then allowed that
   The Senator was right,
For the two-hundred weighted member
   Was certainly in sight.
That puffing corporosity
   Jumped back upon his feet—
" Mr. Speaker—Mr. Speaker—
   Mr. Speaker, I repeat
That according to the letter
   Of what the Senate rulings say,
If a member doesn't cast his vote—
   Why, per se, he is away! "

Uncle Samuel roared aloud :
   " If that ain't climbin' on the fence :

"Mr Speaker, – Mr Speaker, – Mr Speaker," –

Good Lord—Good Lord, please send that chap
  Jest a ray o' common sense ! "
That expansive member thought
  He was having splendid fun,
But in a minute more said member
  Was promptly sat upon.
For the Speaker rose and curtly said,
  According to his view,
Not even a Senator can be
  Both in sight and absent, too.
Next a member who had risen
  To make a short remark,
Took up all the Senate's time
  Till 'twas pretty nearly dark.
Meanwhile Uncle Sam was talking
  With a lad of scarce eighteen,
Who had found a seat beside him,
  But whom before he hadn't seen.
At first they talked of this and that,
  Crops, accidents, and then

They did exchange a view or two
  About their fellow men.
When, growing confidential,
  The young lad said he knew,
He could run a government ''better'n
  What these chaps seem to do.''
And remarking he was tired
  Of all their stupid stuff,
The young man said he guessed he'd go
  For he had had enough.
With a jaunty ''So long!''
  And a most mannerly ''Good day,''
The young man went toward the door;
  But as he strode away,
Uncle Sam—who had forgotten earth
  And every other clime—
Bethought him to investigate
  The locality of time.
He jerked his big gold chain out;
  'Twas exactly half-past five.

"Gee! I'll miss my supper this trip
  As sure as I'm alive!"
He jumped up in a hurry;
  "Now, gen'rally I don't care,
But after goin' through this mill,
  Ye can't be livin' upon air!"
Yet ere he fairly reached the door,
  He gave a backward glance—
One last fond farewell—when
  Toward the front he saw advance
A stately man upon whose brow
  Sat dignity and pride,
A very noble Roman seemed he
  (To judge him from outside)
"Wal, now," said Uncle Samuel,
  "I guess I'd better stay,
For this here feller looks as if
  He'd got somethin' big to say:
I kinder think that his remarks 'll
  Be more pinted, pat and few,

For he seems to know exactly
    What he's startin' out to do.''
So Uncle Samuel went back
    And resumed his former place,
As that Senator began to speak
    With a most impressive grace.
Now, you cannot judge a donkey
    From the mildness of his eyes;
You cannot always tell a storm
    From the signs within the skies;
A rattlesnake looks placid
    When he's basking in the sun;
And you'll never know an orator
    'Till his orating's done.
That noble Roman started in
    And with most pacific mien,
Tried to tell the Senate what his views
    Had ever always been;
He said it grieved him to the heart
    To look about and see,

So many·signs of·discord
And so much perplexity.
But if they'd listen to him—
And he'd try to make them hear—
He would clarify the subject
Till 'twas most opaquely clear,
It ill became a patriot, he thought,
And a Senator indeed,
To sit and never give his views
When his country was in need.
Thus that noble Roman did begin
In a placid even tone,
Which in the not far future
Became a little like a drone;
But it was very even,
And his voice was very clear,
So it sounded very pleasant
For a while to sit and hear;
But slowly Uncle Samuel
As he listened to him speak,

Began to feel so hungry
  That it fairly made him weak;—
"Wal, now I've started out to see
  This 'ere session through—
And I s'pose that feller 'll shut up
  In a minute more or two,
But if he don't, by thunder,
  I hev' got to have a bite,
For my stomach,—wal, my stomach
  Don't feel jest exactly right!"
But when the orator kept on—
  Lo, there came a happy thought,
Uncle Sam remembered that
  As he entered he had bought,
A half a dozen apples.
  How his keen grey eyes did gloat,
As he pulled those rosy apples
  From the pocket of his coat,
And being one who had been reared
  On light and simple fare,

Uncle Samuel seized said apples
    And munched them then and there.
And when the last one was consumed
    Unto the very core,
Though he looked much disappointed
    Because there were no more,
He smacked his lips as every
    Healthy apple-eater does,
And sighed in mild contentment;
    "I am better than I wuz!"
Again he looked down on the floor
    Where in dignified state,
That noble orator still stood
    Ekeing out the great debate;—
"It beats the deuce," said Uncle Sam,
    "The kinds o' human natures;
That feller'd sot down 'fore he riz
    If he know'd pertaters!"
But the noble Roman in his heart
    Held quite another view—

For he talked and talked and talked
    With no sign of getting through;
Came six o'clock,—then seven
    And eight and nine and ten;
Still he stood calmly talking
    To that squad of sleepy men.
Eleven o'clock came in due time,
    But slowly, calmly still
That flood of talk moved like the flow
    Of a patent water-mill.
Then charmed as by some subtle,
    Dunciadic wand or rod,
First beginning to be drowsy,—
    Next to yawn and gape and nod
And with that voice still droning
    Like the moaning of the deep,
Uncle Sam fell into a weary,
    Dreary and exhausted sleep.

UNCLE SAM'S SLEEP.

He slept in peace. But presently—
    Perhaps a half an hour—
He saw the member make an end
    And giving up the floor
Retire in stolid silence
    From the sigh enladen air,
Down through rows of placid faces
    That beamed from everywhere.
Then came a rustle,—during which
    He saw from where he sat,
A tall, quick fellow enter,
    Decked in a cockade hat;
His coat was velvet and his vest
    Was bright in all degrees;
His shoes had silver buckles
    And his pants stopped at the knees;
He wore a sort o' woman's waist
    With ruffles in full view,

While his raven hair was—a la Chinese—
  Done up in a queue;
Yet with a certain antique look
  He carried with him there,
A modest, clear, straightforward
  And a most commanding air.
So wild was Uncle Sam to hear him
  That he could scarcely wait:
" By the shades o' Bunker Hill
  Thet's Patrick Henry sure as fate!
Gosh! But see them sparks o' light
  Ablazin' from his eye;
Now he's the sort o' feller,
  God has made to speechify!"
Uncle Sam then saw he held
  A riding whip in hand, .
But looked as if there was something
  He didn't understand;
He saw him gaze up at the ceiling;
  Then around and all about.

As if in the air was something
He couldn't just make out;
Meanwhile another member rose
And in words that sounded wise,
Said something about Silver
And the need of compromise;
That for the sake of harmony,
He thought it was the better way;
- · For even the side that knew 'twas right
To try and give way;
Because each party needed
To retain its party friends,
Thus, hedging was the proper means
Of gaining governmental ends;
And since nobody was quite
Sure of anything—he guessed
That compromise would be the way—
" For what's safest, that is best!"
And said member who had spoken
In behalf of compromise,

Sat down alooking tickled
  From his boots up to his eyes.
Then Uncle Samuel saw him
  Of the antique coat and queue,
Advance and ask the speaker
  If he could say a word or two:
The drowsy speaker never oped
  His dreamy eyes to peep,
But nodded yes, and then straightway
  Fell off again to sleep.
He smiled—did Patrick Henry—
  At men sleeping 'neath his view;
He smiled as if to say: " I guess
  You'll wake up before I'm through!"
But he proceeded to explain
  In a very quiet tone,
Where since last time Congress met,
  Where it was that he had gone;
He said he went to Charlotteville
  To consult with Thomas J;

And that indeed he didn't think
That he'd be so long away,—
To tell the whole truth after
His long riding he was glad
To return,—especially
As the roads were very bad;
Then he stated—while his voice
Rose in volume and in vim—
That whereas the present question
Was a little new to him,
And as he was quite unprepared
He wouldn't speak on it to-day;
But that however there was one thing
Which he felt impelled to say,—
For his heart down to its very depths
With sorrow had been stirred,
By the low, vile, petty sophistry
Of the things he had just heard.

"Look at the Lessons of the Past—and they lie in easy reach—
Look at Earth's dead empires, what do their bitter records teach?
What says the glories of old Rome, what says her dying sighs?
This,—that human Right and Wrong can hold no compromise!
Do you ever think that ever since the very birth of Time,
Through all the mournful ages stained with folly, blood and
      crime,
That where a single fact has risen from darkness into light,
'Tis because a deed was done there just because 'twas right:
That all else is forgotten! Not a man to-day can tell,
The names of mightiest influence for whom great Nations fell,
The rich, the powerful, and all the worldly-wise,
Who by schemes and cliques, and combinations showed their
      enterprise
All dead and unremembered as the dullest piece of clay,
For Sophistry shall perish do whatsoe'er it may.
And as for statesmen's records, I think you'll find it true—
Fearless minds have made the many, and tricks have made
      the few;
'Tis small two-penny thinkers who follow the wise ends
Of making God Almighty serve the views of their dear friends;
Who think they manage Fortune, or what is rather worse,
Who fancy their potato patch is the mighty Universe.

Sir, the Nation—the whole Nation! That and that alone
      should be.

The sign, the guide, the watchword of a statesman's loyalty.
Whatsoever State shall rise in strength, intelligence and might,
Must rest upon the rock foundations of eternal right;
For if a Nation is to keep its corpse above the sod,
It first must try to live in harmony with God.
It's the vilest sort of falsehood that's been spoken here to-day.
'Tis not the policy that's safe which is the wisest way.
Sir, I say to all assembled here, by the blue eternal skies,
That the man or State which tampers with the jugglery of lies,
As sure as Night shall follow Day,—That man or nation dies!"

As Patrick Henry took his seat,
    Came a sudden breathless lull,
And next a round of sharp applause
    Which filled the Senate full—
Applause which slowly rose into
    A loud re-echoing roar,
That sounded like the storm surf
    Beating on a rocky shore.
The sleepy heads were all awake;
    Here and there and everywhere
Men were stamping, clapping, shouting--
    Nay! the very air

Seemed to fairly flame with fire
   Like a glowing sunset sky,
With a splendor that has caught ablaze
   From a single human eye.
Uncle Sam got so excited
   That he swung his old plug hat,
As he murmured: "Gee! I wish that I
   Could speechify like that!"
An opinion in which, by the way,
   All seemed undivided,
Therefore it took some minutes
   Ere the Senators subsided—
For although men in words will wrangle—
   Grow rosy and perspire,
They all unite at once upon
   What compels them to admire,
Now when the Senate had resumed
   Its former gentle state,
Of quiet and innocuous
   Desuetudinous debate,

The Speaker, he arose and said:
" There was present with them there
A gentleman of fame known through
    The Nation everywhere,
An active legislator, too—
    Though that was long ago—
For of late years he had rather
    Been an ex-officio;
However, it occurred to him
    That perhaps it might pay
For the Senators to listen
    To what he had to say
About the general problems
    And questions of the day;
And would the following Senators
    (Naming three of reverend age),
Conduct their Uncle Samuel
    Up to the Speaker's stage.
As Uncle Sam heard that he saw
    A (Silver) member scoot;

And looking toward the door he thought
  He'd better follow suit;
Just then those Senators came up
  And with a pleasant smile,
Conducted him in frigid silence
  Down that awful lengthy aisle;
His head it swum; his vision reeled;
  It seemed that he was blind,
When of a sudden Patrick Henry
  Arose before his mind,
And after that he never felt
  The tiniest bit afraid,
But stood right up—and all alone—
  And this is what he said:

UNCLE SAM'S SPEECH.

"Feller Countrymen, it is with great pleasure that I rise,
To stand upon this Senate floor, and to look into ye're eyes:
I hev' often heard about ye, and I'm very glad to say,
That I feel exceedin' interest in bein' here to-day.
Though with all ye're modern notions I cannot jest agree,
I tell ye they're chuck full o' quanderies fur me;—

Here and there I kinder thought I ketched onto a pint,
That seemed to me as if 'twas yanked a little out o' jint;
So when I kin manage to collect the gist o' my ideas,
I'd like to tell ye some few things that the farmer feller sees:
If I'm too brief in my remarks, please forgit my failin's for
I wasn't brought up in my youth to be no orator;
I'm jest a plain old fashioned chap thet wants his land to be
A place where common kind o' folks kin live happy and live free.
Where the hul' concern kin revel in the best o' human health,
And, by mindin' their own bizness kin get on the road to wealth.
Where Tom and Dick and Harry aire as good as you and me—
Previded thet they're loyal to our old Ameriky;
And if they ain't—I hevn't nary hide nor hair o' doubt,
That we'd better riz together and proceed to throw them out;
Or rather—though perhaps it's somewhat latish to begin,
We'd better see 'bout lettin' so many cartloads in.
Howsomever, I won't specialize about this thing or that,—
I want to mention what I think this country's comin' at;—
We're a mighty big concern I 'low and yit it seems to me
Our Constitooshun ain't exactly what it used to be;
Or rather I should mention thet the way thet things aire run,
Ain't precisely what they wuz in the days o' Washington.
Fur politics strike me as a great big game o' grab;
With the prizes for the fellers with the biggest gift o' gab;
And the question nowdays ain't so much to do the thing thet's
    right

As to keep a swimmin' in the swim and look purty and perlite;
Now I wouldn't like to tread upon anybody's feelin's,
But I really think you hev' too many underhanded dealin's;
And I wouldn't say thet any on' ye'd go startin' out to shirk,—
But what makes ye spend a week on a middlin' fair day's work?
It's a fact ye take a heap o' time according to my view,
In consultin' round instead of doin' what you started out to do;
Though you all look mighty chipper and mighty hale and hearty.
When the question to be settled is agoin' to suit your party!
Oh I've watched your ways and doin's till I know ye to a T.
I'm a plain old country hayseed, but ye can't bamboozle me."

'Twas hereabouts that Uncle Sam
    Thought he heard a haw and hem,
And someone say they didn't want
    No old fool to lecture them ;
Then a member rose up with a gaze
    Of most pathetic scorn—
(For his mind looked as if it might
    Be suffering from a corn)—
" I rise to point of order,
    And I say it with great pain

That the member's statement of the facts
Is too shockingly plain "—

"Damnation take your indirections"—turning with a whiz—
"The trouble with you fellers.—the trouble with you is—
You've lost all sense and meanin' of good old honest biz;
To do a thing because its right and because its fair and square;
To act as ye think ye orter and stand for what you aire:
Instid o' thet, 'bout all you do when you're startin' out to vote,
Is to peek around to see the color o' the other feller's coat,—
What party he belongs to,—as if it matter'd one blamed cop-
        per cent;
Kin ye find two kinds o' patriots in a loyal government?
What party!—Better drowned your parties in the old Atlantic
        ocean,
And then sit down and try to git some decent kind o' notion,
O' what your duties to your Nation and your homeland ought
        to be,
I tell ye, Freedom's cause ain't helped by the schemers thet
        ye see!
When they wuz born, half on 'em should been laid back on
        the shelf;
A statesman thinks of somethin' besides his pocket and himself."

As Uncle Sam stepped from the stage,
He saw a crowd of men

Come up to offer their good wishes
To which he smiled, and then—
He woke up with a sudden jerk
Like one risen from the dead,
The speech still ringing in his ears
Of all (he imagined) he had said ;
Just where or what he was
He couldn't exactly see,
For instead of being on the floor,
He was in the gallery.
Beside him stood a fleshy man
Whose garments did encase,
A form that was as plump and rotund
As his rotund face ;
Uncle Sam looked up and queried—
"Wal, an' who be you ?"
That rotund person gave one look
That froze him through and through.
As with a cry of indignation
He called out with a roar—

"I? You poor old ignoramus—
  I am the Janitor!"
"I beg your pardon, mister,
  But I never did pretend
To recognize too sudden
  Even my bosomest friend;
Now jedgin' in a gin'ral way
  From your independent bent,
I didn't know but what ye might
  Hev' bin the President."
The Janitor, he smiled and
  In milder fashion said,
He might be some day, but meanwhile
  He'd do cleanin' up instead;
Then with a curious expression
  Which certainly seemed queer,
He added: "It's time, I reckon,
  You were gettin' out o' here!"

That capped the climax! Uncle Sam
  Was now all in a daze,

He stretched himself back in his chair,
  And muttered in a maze : —
" Gee ! I don't see where I be ;
  Wal, I've got my hat ;
But where's Patrick Henry gone ?
  An' geewhittaker ! whose that ? "
He saw a sight that struck him dumb—
  Could it be that he was ill ?
That same old droning orator
  Was down there droning still;
Then suddenly he was possessed
  By a fearful inward fright,
" Whew! I never knew before
  My head wa'n't exactly right—"
He rushed up to the Janitor
  (Who was smiling with delight)
" Where'd thet fellow come from?"
  Pointing through the morning light,
" Why he's the tedious idiot
  That's been talking here all night!"

"'Goodness bless me! then—then
  I ain't crazy after all;
Wal, wal, (he murmured) but I've
  Been shook up powerful!"
Then he saw it all—how instead
  Of speeches dire and deep,
He had merely been indulging
  In a Senatorial sleep;
But he didn't feel quite rested—
  For into his hearing still,
Came that weary, dreary droning
  Of that patent water-mill;
The Senator of placid·voice
  Was still trying to give as news
Unto his weary colleagues,
  His twice told tedious views;
At last, as there's an end even
  To what a mill-wheel can repeat,
'Mid grateful sighs of glad relief
  That member took his seat.

Next a member who had risen
 And secured the floor,
(A man he was who'd spoken
 Five separate times before)
Gave notice he could end his speech
 If they gave him two days more;
Another Senator arose,
 And with charming modesty,
Said that as for days to end his speech,
 He needed only three.
Then, after two more members
 Had taken their modest turn,
The Speaker called out for a vote,
 And the Senate did adjourn.
For the Speaker said that after
 Sitting up all night he guessed,
They'd agree with him that there was need
 Of a little solid rest ;
Scarce a minute did elapse
 After work was ended there,

They found themselves outside
  In the good fresh morning air ;
Then, as in his stomach Uncle Sam
  Was feeling rather gaunt,
He betook himself straightway unto
  The nearest restaurant ;
And he murmured slowly as he
  Plodded meekly on his way :
" Gee ! But I've learned a heap
  Since this time yistiddy."

THE END.